A Random Walk Down Abercorn & Habersham Streets

(A Savannah Tour Guide)

John H. Maclean

Copyright © 2020 by John H. Maclean

All rights reserved. No part of this publication may be reproduced, distributed or transmitted in any form or by any means, including photocopying, recording or other electronic or mechanical methods, without the prior written permission of the publisher, except in the case of brief quotations embodied in reviews and certain other non-commercial uses permitted by copyright law.

Printed in the United States of America
Print ISBN: 978-1-951490-86-7
E-Book ISBN: 978-1-951490-87-4

Canoe Tree Press
4697 Main Street
Manchester Center, VT 05255

Canoe Tree Press is a division of
of DartFrog Books

www.CanoeTreePress.com

*To my mother, Frances Ravenel Maclean,
who gave Savannah her allegiance
while keeping Charleston close to her heart.*

Contents

Preface

This is a companion book to *A Random Walk Down Bull Street.* Savannah was the largest city in Georgia until around 1875. Whatever happened here meant it happened in Georgia. If Bull Street is described as the heart of Savannah, then Abercorn can best be described as the hearth and home of the City. It is the street on which old large homes were built for the wealthy and enterprising "Merchant Princes."

The purpose of this book is to describe what went on around these houses and Squares and give some historical context to them. If some of the old homes have returned to dust, Savannah has held on to others like a locket to her breast. Each generation holds its past in trust for the future. Sometimes you just have to close your eyes to see, by feeling the past like a breeze against your face.

Before you begin you must understand an underlying truth about Savannah that is known at birth, but rarely spoken openly. The county is not Chatham, but the "Free State of Chatham." Georgia only exists to serve Savannah. Even the New York Times once said "Savannah has always seen itself as a semi-autonomous republic in relation to the rest of the state..." This is not an exaggeration. Indeed, if you go out to Tybee Island you will find those folks believe they are a separate country.

A Random Walk Down Abercorn Street

As in the companion book, we start from the top at Reynolds Square and randomly walk our way down Abercorn toward Forsyth Park and end at Calhoun Square. The street itself was named after the Earl of Abercorn, an early financial supporter of the Colony.

The Earl most likely met Tomochichi when he visited London as shown by this 1735 painting by William Verelst.

Audience given by the trustees of Georgia
to a delegation of Creek Indians
Photo credit: Georgia Historical Society

Reynolds Square

Reynolds Square was one of the first Squares to be established after Johnson Square. It was named for James Reynolds, the first Royal Governor of Georgia who served in the 1750's. The colonists intensely disliked him and had him replaced. The Square is bracketed by the streets Abercorn and Congress with St. Julien intersecting. St. Julien was a South Carolina friend of the colony so he got a street. This Square, like almost all, had a well in the middle and was surrounded by a fence with a turnstile for entrance. The turnstile kept horses and cows from entering.

In the middle of the Square is a statue of John Wesley, the founder of Methodism and one of the first rectors of Christ Church on Johnson Square. He and his brother came to Savannah in the 1730's. His first sermon was from 1st Corinthians and given at a public building on the current site of the Customs House at Bull and Bay streets in March 1736. His brother tried to convert the Indians, failed and went back to England. John then got mixed up with a young woman whom he courted then denied her church services when she rejected his advances. He was eventually run out of town so this statue always seems a little odd. His parsonage was on this

Square. He later got religion and founded Methodism when he went back home to England.

The Colony started out being run by Trustees with General Oglethorpe as the onsite manager. After 20 years the management became difficult so they turned the Colony over to the Crown. Reynolds was the first Royal Governor, arriving in 1754. Reynolds was not very popular. Reynolds Square was the location of colonial government and originally held the House of Assembly, where the first reading of the Declaration of Independence took place in Georgia.

So to sum up early Savannah government, they first had Royal Governor Reynolds whom they hated, Ellis whom they liked and Wright whom they arrested. Then they had a revolution. You just can't please everyone.

When setting up the Colony the Trustees had to sell the King on granting them a charter. One of their sales pitches was that they would grow silk so he wouldn't have to get it from Italy. On this Square was the Filature which was a large building for separating the silk from the silkworms. The Filature was on the Trust Lot facing the Square and bounded by Abercorn, St. Julian, Lincoln and Bryan Streets. At some point the Corp of Engineers built a large red brick building on this trust lot which was then restored by a law firm.

Before you think Savannah has a street named after President Lincoln, it is actually named for General Benjamin Lincoln who not only failed to recapture Savannah from the British in 1779, but then went on to surrender Charleston to them as well! So his failure was honored with a street. He partially redeemed himself at Yorktown. When Cornwallis refused to attend the surrender ceremony faking illness and sending in his second-in-command,

Washington refused to accept Cornwallis' sword, but had his second-in-command General Lincoln accept it.

The silk idea soon failed as the worm cocoons did not grow well in Georgia, but the large Filature building remained and was used for a meeting house and city hall. When President George Washington visited Savannah in 1791, he was honored with a large dance held in this building. He says in his diary that he was introduced to "100 well dressed and handsome ladies." They danced to several minuets and a country dance and then Washington was exhausted and went home at 11pm. The ladies danced until three in the morning.

It also served as a playhouse and in 1783 the tragedy, *The Fair Penitent* was performed. The advertisement for this and other plays made it quite clear that "... no gentlemen will be admitted behind the scenes on any pretense." Even back then, Savannah was a proper young lady.

In 1813 Savannah believed that the British were about to invade and established Fort Jackson and stationed troops in the city. The city turned the Filature into a hospital for those troops. British Admiral Cockburn, who had burned the White House and Capitol, landed soldiers on Cumberland Island in 1815, but did not come any closer to Savannah.

Savannah has had several large fires, which have swept through the city destroying vast sections (1796, 1820— 463 buildings from Bay to Broughton, 1865 and 1889). However, on Reynolds Square there exist two homes that have survived all these calamities.

The first house of note is **The Pink House** which was originally the Habersham House. It was built on this Trust Lot in 1771 by James Habersham, Jr. who came from an old Savannah family. The pink stucco gives it its name. This pink shade was originally caused by the red brick bleeding through the white plaster when built. Houses facing Squares are on Trust Lots, which were originally quite large.

The house was scheduled for demolition in the 1930's when Alida Harper saved it and turned it into a tearoom. Alida Harper was a truly remarkable woman who was way ahead of her time in saving and restoring these old houses. She restored ten houses in all, including this one. Her home is now called the **Harper-Fowlkes (McAlpin) House** and is at 230 Barnard Street on Orleans Square and is open to visitors. Her house there was built in Greek Revival style in 1842 and currently serves as the head-quarters for the *Society of the Cincinnati* in the State of Georgia. The history of preservation in Savannah is filled with women who sought to save, preserve and protect. A hotel is named in her honor.

The Pink House features a nice Greek portico with a wonderful Palladian window above and a fanlight over the front door. The original owner, James Habersham, Jr., broke with his father over the Colonial Rebellion as his father supported the Crown. This may have been due to his liberal Princeton education. His father was probably the wealthiest person in the Georgia Colony owning vast rice plantations and many slaves. He also exported the first bales of cotton in 1764.

The Olde Pink House
Photo Credit: The Placencia Group

Habersham's father was a strong proponent of ending the prohibition against slavery in the Colony as he saw how wealthy the South Carolina colonists had become from rice planting. Indeed his father's firm of Harris and Habersham imported hundreds of slaves direct from Gambia. One of his father's business partners, Deane, was the Captain of a British owned slave ship and lived with an African woman, who had also been a slave trader, and their children at Lebanon Plantation across the river from Savannah. Deane's career came to an explosive end in 1772 when his African crew gave the slaves on board tools to free themselves who then attacked the crew. In the fighting, the ship's magazine detonated killing all but Deane and one other.

Ironically, James Jr.'s son Richard, who was born in this house, became the US Attorney for Georgia and in 1820 prosecuted the men of the *Antelope*, a slave running ship that had violated the 1808 law against importation of slaves. The case took several trips to the US Supreme

Court before 120 slaves were freed and sent back to Africa. The famous Francis Scott Key argued the case for their freedom before the Supreme Court on behalf of the United States.

*James Habersham, the father; portrait 1772
by Jeremiah Theus; original at Telfair*

James Jr. held meetings of the Sons of Liberty at his house. His brother Joseph was a Son of Liberty, arrested the Royal Governor James Wright, and participated in the raid on the powder magazine, some of which ended up at the Battle of Bunker Hill. If his father had not died in 1775, family dinners would have been awkward.

James, along with his brother, was a member of the first Board of Trustees establishing the University of Georgia in 1785. You could call him the "First Dawg." He was also an early cotton factor. James died in 1799 and with his father and brothers reside in Colonial Park Cemetery. Supposedly his ghost wanders around the bar area of the Pink House restaurant so you may catch sight of him yet.

The storied surname of Habersham, original to the Colony, would die out due to the Civil War. Of seven sons born to Josephine Habersham, two would die in infancy, another at age 7, and two at ages 20 and 21 at the battle of Atlanta on the same day. Of the two boys who remained only one had a child, a daughter. The daughters did have children and their descendants are sprinkled about the fair city, but the surname is dust in the wind. *Sic transit mundus*

In 1812 the Habersham "Pink House" became the location of the Planters Bank. In 1865 it was the headquarters of the Provost Marshall, Brigadier General York. It was here that Confederate women came to beg for more time when ordered to leave the city in the middle of a very cold March 1865. York was sympathetic, but his boss, the vindictive General Grover was not. In the 1880's my Great grandmother's first cousin had his law office in this building.

The Square became a venue for all sorts of different types of entertainment. In *The Georgian* on May 11, 1820, it was advertised that in the Square, across from the bank would be shown a lion and her cub, a Brazilian tiger, and an African leopard for only 50 cents. Most of the Squares in the 19th Century, including Reynolds, held a cistern holding water for the fire department.

Later in that century there was a dangerous confluence of animals and machines. On October 26, 1893, a tricycle went off the sidewalk on East Broad and struck a parked horse and buggy frightening the animal. The animal with buggy took off with the tricycle stuck in its wheels down Congress toward Reynolds Square "at breakneck speed." Upon reaching Reynolds Square the horse was frightened even more by an electric car, ran into a sulky causing that horse to break its harness and take off. Meanwhile our runaway had leapt in the air, losing the buggy and striking an elderly woman standing on the curb. As she was taken away unconscious to the hospital it was not known if she would live. This mixture of horses, buggies, sulkies, bicycles, electric cars and streetcars all made downtown an exciting, but dangerous place.

Earlier in the century Savannah had even stranger locomotion issues. General Tom Thumb, of Barnum and Bailey, made an appearance in February 1851 at Oglethorpe Hall located at the corner of Drayton and Bay streets. General Thumb advertised that he would perform songs and dances including representations of Napoleon, Frederick the Great and Greek statuary. He would wear elegant court dress and Highland costumes. This visit to the city occurred after he appeared before Queen Victoria. Apparently he was riding along in his goat carriage on Oglethorpe Avenue when it veered off onto the sidewalk frightening pedestrians. He was arrested and brought up before the Magistrate. He was only fined $10 as it was deemed a small affair.

GEN. TOM THUMB,

THE WONDERFUL MAN IN MINIATURE, weighing only 15 pounds, eighteen years of age, and but 28 inches high, who has been received with the highest marks of royal favor by Queen Victoria, and all the principal crowned heads and nobility of Europe, and has appeared before 7,000,000 of persons during the past eight years, will hold his Levees at Oglethorpe Hall, Savannah, Monday, Tuesday and Wednesday, Feb. 17, 18, and 19. Positively for three days only.

Hours of exhibition——afternoons, from 3 1-2 to 5 o'clock; evenings, from 7 1-2 to 9. Doors open half an hour in advance.

The General will appear in all his beautiful and amusing performances, including SONGS and DANCES, representations of Napoleon, Frederick the Great, Grecian Statuary in costume, his various elegant Court Dresses, Highland Costume, &c. &c. His magnificent presents and jewellery will be exhibited in the hall.

His beautiful MINIATURE EQUIPAGE, presented by Queen Victoria, may be seen in front of the Hall at the close of each day's levee.

Admission, 25 cents; no half price.

feb 13   6

You may hear that Sherman did not burn Savannah as he did Atlanta and Columbia, but that is only technically true. In January 1865, a month after Sherman first occupied the city, a huge fire broke out near the intersection of West Broad Street (MLK Blvd.) and Broughton Street in a stable near Granite Hall where Confederate ammunition was stored. The fire swept through the town burning over 100 buildings in that area. It was described as having flames leaping high in the air thrown up by exploding thirteen-inch shells. It may have been caused by one of the occupying soldiers. Yet this house and the Sturges one survived.

Next to The Pink House is the **Oliver Sturges House** at 27 Abercorn Street on the location of John Wesley's Parsonage. It was built in 1813. Sturges, along with Scarborough, was part owner of SS Savannah, the first steamship to cross the Atlantic. It is said that it was in the parlor room that the plans for the crossing by the SS Savannah were first made.

Just prior to its voyage President Monroe came to visit and had dinner on board. The SS Savannah was the first side wheeler steamer to cross the Atlantic and did so in 1819. It traveled as far as St. Petersburg, Russia before returning home. It was considered powerful at 90 horse-power. Before that time steamers were coastal vessels never moving much out of sight of land. Even the SS Savannah traveled mostly under sail for the majority of the voyage. The ship had no passengers as people were afraid steamers would blow up. This venture was not a financial success.

The next steamers to cross the Atlantic occurred in 1838 almost 20 years later. Many steamships into the late 19th Century still carried sail when crossing the ocean. Savannah would not see commercial side wheeler steam-ships entering her harbor until 1848.

SS Savannah painting by Hunter Wood; note smokestack and side wheel

Sturges was obviously wealthy so he showed that off by not using the softer local Savannah grey brick, but rather imported harder red brick and laid them in a Flemish bond style of a header followed by a stretcher. This was a more expensive way to do it.

In an interesting note, the famous escaped slave William Grimes served as a carriage driver for Sturges for a time. Grimes wrote the first narrative by an ex-slave in 1825 while living in New Haven, Connecticut. His story, *William Grimes, the Runaway Slave* is available online.

On the edge of the property in the flagstone sidewalk is a sewer inlet with the date of 1872 clearly shown. The sidewalk then moved further out so the inlet is now closer to the current street along a granite curb. Granite curbs are typical of Savannah. The trees along the original sidewalk are in what is called a "tree lawn." When Savannah began to pave its very wide streets for automobiles, it did not pave the whole street but saved money by only paving what was necessary. Many streets had trees in the middle so they simply changed from having trees in the middle to having them next to the original sidewalk. Liberty and Oglethorpe streets illustrate the old design with trees in the middle.

For those who enjoy reading architectural tea leaves, the parking lot behind the Sturges House offers up clues to the past. In the rear next to Drayton Street is the faint imprint outline of a triangle shaped carriage house. Next to it is a one brick thick house leading to a garden arch with a filled in door. It is like looking at a photographic negative, except it's a negative of a building.

Next door to the Sturges House on the left was an identical home owned by Sturges' partner Benjamin Burroughs. They were called "mirror" houses. The partners shipped a large load of cotton on the SS Savannah on its maiden voyage to Liverpool.

At 18 Abercorn St. is the **Christ Church Parish House** where I had Sunday school as a boy and it is still used like that today. It was built in 1911 for the Leroy Myers Cigar Company that dealt in Havana tobacco. On top of the building is a 12th Century weathervane from England. The Christ Church minister when I was growing up was a very spiritual man named Dr. Tucker. His mother was the last child to grow up at George Washington's Mount Vernon.

Until 1850 the city used whale oil lamps to illuminate the streets. These were placed at the water pumps in the middle of the squares and at intersections. These lamps were not very effective and so most people did not go out at night. If they did, they would carry their own lantern. It was not unusual to have cows out and about sleeping anywhere and as people walked in the darkness a large shape would suddenly appear rising in front of them. After 1850 pipes were laid and gas was used to light the city's lamps. After 1883 electricity was used.

There was an ordinance concerning the cow problem, but it was not always enforced. On November 20, 1878, a woman was attacked in Reynolds Square by "one of these manufacturers of the lacteal fluid" and "might have been seriously injured but for the timely interference of a gentleman who was passing." The very next day Mrs. Crean was attacked on President Street by "a vicious cow" and was chased with the animal "tearing her shawl and umbrella to pieces." The newspaper said the police were now taking up the cows and impounding them.

The Squares on Abercorn during the late 19th Century

were generally used as parks and had fences around them. In 1871 the Legislature allowed streetcars to run through the middle and Savannahians were outraged. The case went up to the Georgia Supreme Court which ruled for the streetcar company. Little boys would play in Reynolds Square and occasionally get run over by the streetcar as happened to 6 year old David Hall on May 3, 1888. As a boy I used to see fire engines race through the middle. Luckily all that is now outlawed, but in 1920 they even tried to run the street through Colonial Cemetery!

Reynolds Square in 1930 with streetcar tracks

By 1890 baseball was all the rage and was played in Reynolds Square. One homeowner was irate and said in June that the Mayor should do something about the "small army of young men and boys [who] gather there frequently and make life for them almost unbearable by their noise and indecent language."

Also found near Reynolds Square is the **Lucas Theater** located at 22 Abercorn Street. It is built on the site of the old Houstoun-Screven house and its garden. Houstoun was the first Governor of Georgia before the British reclaimed the city in late December 1778.

The Lucas by Ebyabe

The Houstoun-Screven house was typical of its day. Since there was no central heat, each room in one of these grand houses had access to a hard coal fire that would burn all day during the winter. The fire would be started by a blower which increased the draught. The story goes that at one house they were training a country girl to be a house maid and she just couldn't seem to grasp the concept of the blower. Finally, the owner got so exasperated that he just said, "use you head girl, use your head." The next day he smelled something burning and found the poor girl on all fours with her head butting the blower in place and her hair scorched!

Breakfast at this house would be a large affair eaten on a grand mahogany dining table with silver service. Dinner was at 2:00 then a customary nap followed by a trip back to the office.

The Lucas Theater was built in 1921 for Arthur Lucas and was one of the first air-conditioned theaters in the country. It was originally designed both for silent films and vaudeville and was eventually updated for "talkies." A Buster Keaton comedy and a Rudolph Valentino movie were the first two films shown. In 1920 Valentino actually starred in a silent movie filmed in Savannah at the grand Shotter mansion next to Bonaventure Cemetery. The Shotter mansion burned down in a fire in 1923 and was considered as fine as the Biltmore.

The theater closed in 1976 and was to be demolished and turned into a parking lot. After great effort the theater was saved and restored. During restoration it appeared in an episode of *This Old House*. The theater has some amazing decorative features in the style you would expect from a 1920's theater. To help raise funds for the restoration, Clint Eastwood sold tickets to the wrap party held here for his movie *Midnight in the Garden of Good and Evil*. When the theater reopened in 2000, the first movie shown was appropriately *Gone with the Wind.* Across Abercorn from the Lucas were two other theatres, the Bijou and Odeon. It was theater corner!

Across from the Houstoun-Screven House (the present Lucas) on the corner of Abercorn and Congress was the Mackay house where General Robert E. Lee would visit many times when he stayed in Savannah as a young man. He and John Mackay were at West Point together. The house was torn down to make way for a movie theater in the late 1930's.

Mackay House

It was from here that the Mackay women and children watched the Union Army roll into town coming up Abercorn to Bay Street. They then marched west on Bay Street in parade formation. The servants were ordered to keep the shutters closed, but through a few slats that were opened they could see a "pouring...sea of blue-coated soldiers, shouting, leaping, and brandishing their muskets." One young girl at the house was later told by her mother "how the loose women of the town rushed out in the streets to welcome the Yankees, kissing and embracing them, and dancing in an abandon of joy."

The invaders left the Mackay house alone for the most part although they did break into the wine cellar that held bottles of Madeira. What they could not steal they simply destroyed. This was a fairly common occurrence during the Occupation. No liquor stash was safe from the Union's "bummers."

Street sellers would walk down Broughton in front of the Mackay house and all the others crying out "Cra-ab Buyer here!" "Swimp Buyer here!" On their heads they would carry round flat baskets filled with crabs and shrimp.

In the 1840's on the northwest corner of Abercorn and Broughton (currently Broughton Municipal Building) was an old building where Miss Church had her elementary school. Miss Church was a typical New England schoolmarm. The children used goose quills which she would carve in front of them. The curriculum consisted of Webster's Spelling Book, a small geography book showing Texas, California and the West as belonging to Mexico, and Oklahoma, Nebraska and such described as the "Great American Desert." There was also a "Child's History of the United States," which was primarily about Plymouth Rock. Charles Olmstead, who later surrendered Fort Pulaski to the Union, was in her class one bright sunny day. He said he saw how nice it was outside, how the breeze was blowing, so he counted to 20, stood up and just ran outside. End of class!

As you cross Broughton Street, to your immediate left is Leopold's Ice Cream, a local ice cream parlor favorite

Oglethorpe Square

Continuing down Abercorn we come upon Oglethorpe Square which was established in 1742 and named for the founder of Georgia. It is located between State and York Streets with President Street intersecting. Prior to the Revolution State Street was called "Prince" and President was "King." York is named after the Duke of York. My great grandmother's father built a very nice house at 205 E. York in 1855 in which he raised 9 children!

Oglethorpe Square is a very shady place to sit and ponder great thoughts. During the Union Occupation soldiers pitched their white tents in the Square. Oglethorpe's monument is not located here, but in Chippewa Square continuing Savannah's grand tradition of never having a monument in the Square of the same name.

At the corner of Abercorn and State is a public garage. On that site used to be Dr. Richard Arnold's house.

Old Arnold House
Photo Credit: Library of Congress

Dr. Arnold was one of Savannah's better leaders. He was educated at the University of Pennsylvania medical school and returned home where he became a newspaper man running the largest daily. Arnold supported the Compromise of 1850 and opposed all cries of *Disunion,* but changed to a secessionist later in the decade. He returned to medicine and during the 1854 yellow fever epidemic led the efforts taking care of the sick and dying.

He was elected Mayor four times and had the misfortune of being the Mayor when General Sherman came to town for a visit at Christmas, 1864. Between the joint efforts of himself and General Geary the city survived the Occupation in fairly good shape. At this house Dr. Arnold entertained the great *Hamlet* actor Edwin Booth, the older brother of John Wilkes Booth, when he came to Savannah for a performance. Edwin was a Union man and was appalled at the actions of his brother. Dr. Arnold was born in this house in 1808 and died in the same room of his birth in 1876 from the last yellow fever epidemic.

On the Square at 124 Abercorn Street may be the most beautiful house in Savannah, the **Owens-Thomas House**. It was designed by William Jay in English Regency style with some Greek Revival elements and erected in 1819. Greek Revival was just beginning to appear in America at the time as a way of showing our democratic heritage. It was one of the first houses in America to have indoor plumbing. Storage tanks would collect rainwater which would travel through pipes to the water closets. The house contains a basement which is actually from an earlier building on the plot and is built of tabby. Tabby was a common building material in the 18th Century made from oyster shells, lime, sand and water.

Owens-Thomas House by Ebyabe

The original owner, Richard Richardson was one of the wealthiest merchants in Savannah and originally from New Orleans. He was partners with the Boltons and subsequently married Frances Bolton. The Boltons also had a house on this Square. Richardson's driver, Andrew Marshall, was the pastor of the First African Baptist Church when it was built on Franklin Square. That church is the oldest continuous active African-American church in America.

Richardson did not get to enjoy the house very long as in January 1820 came the big fire that destroyed three-fourths of Savannah, followed by a Yellow Fever epidemic that killed another thousand, followed by losing his business from the residual effects of the national financial panic of 1819. He also suffered personal tragedy with the deaths of two children and wife in 1822. The house eventually ended up being owned by the bank. Part of Richardson's business included sending slaves down to New Orleans for sale. He perished at sea in 1833 on his way back from France to New Orleans.

The home had become a boarding house by the time the Marquis de Lafayette came to visit on March 19, 1825 at age 67. His visit occurred 48 years after his heroic defense at the Battle of Brandywine. By 1825 he was the last surviving Revolutionary War Major General. A year later on July 4, 1826, both Thomas Jefferson and John Adams would die on the same day. The Old Guard was leaving us. He took rooms in the house on the first floor by President Street and spoke in both French and English to adoring crowds for two hours from the balcony. One of the Chatham Artillery's "Washington Guns" from Yorktown was fired in salute.

The prominent Lamar family also took rooms in the home at the same time as Lafayette. The little baby who would grow up to be Colonel Lamar was christened at this time at Christ Church and Lafayette stood as one of the baby's sponsors. The father and child Lamars would be the only members of their family to survive the 1838 *Pulaski* ship disaster described below. Colonel Lamar would later perish in defense of Columbus, Georgia in 1865 as perhaps his punishment for illegally importing slaves to Jekyll Island in 1858 on his ship the *Wanderer*. His nursemaid "old Mauma Lucy" died in 1887, but always said how she remembered General Lafayette on the occasion of the christening of her charge.

Many toasts were given at the banquet to Lafayette that night at the old City Exchange where City Hall now stands. One was to Lafayette, "The name shall be a badge worn in the hour of peril by freeman in every quarter of the globe when their rights are assailed by oppression." Of course, there was a toast to: "Woman—The graces of her mind refine our manners, the virtues of her heart correct our morals, and civilized man derives his strongest impulse to excellence from the hope of her approbation."

The Governor of South Carolina was not allowed to join the Lafayette festivities as the South Carolina Constitution did not allow the Governor to leave the State. So he was in a little boat tied up across the river and periodically people would row over to him to tell him what was going on.

George Owens, a former mayor and Congressman, bought the house from the bank in 1830 and for the next 121 years his family continued to own it. His granddaughter bequeathed the home to the Telfair Academy in 1951 as a house museum.

These old houses would generally have a large cooking fireplace in the basement toward the rear. The cook would sit in front of it with a *tinder horn* between her knees. The horn was part of a cow's horn and the tinder was scorched cotton. The flint would be in the right hand and the steel in the left then a spark struck off would strike the tinder and light the fat lightwood. Soon you would have a roaring kitchen fire.

The Square contains a small memorial to Moravian missionaries who arrived at the same time as John Wesley and then resettled in Pennsylvania. They were from Saxony and were only in Savannah a short time trying to do missionary work among the Indians in the Yamacraw area before moving on. The group dwindled over time due to political infighting then Quaker-like reluctance to take up arms against the Spanish threat. I really have no idea why we have a memorial here except the Moravians lived near this Square, had a mission site at Broughton and Habersham and were friendly with John Wesley.

Across the Square from the Owens-Thomas House is 123 Abercorn. There used to be a Unitarian Church located here built in 1851. What is interesting is that James Pierpont was the church music director while his brother was the minister. He was later to be the Uncle to the banker and financier James Pierpont Morgan. While he was at this church, James wrote "Jingle Bells," originally published as "One Horse Open Sleigh" in 1857. The family was from Boston and his father was a huge abolitionist.

The history is a little hazy but it appears that while the song was written here, it may have first been performed in Medford, Massachusetts or in Boston as a minstrel. Pierpont went on to write songs for the Confederacy while his father went to work as a chaplain for the Union Army. Like the Habershams, father and son had their awkward differences. His wife's brother was killed at Manassas, the first battle of the Civil War, and Pierpont asked to be buried next to him in Laurel Grove Cemetery and so he lies, Jingling on to his reward.

Oglethorpe Square was also not without its "mad cow" problems as one got loose from a herd being driven through the city in March 1903. It was not unusual for a small herd to be driven down Bay Street from the railroad yard on the west side to the Screven ferry landing on the east. The wild cow knocked a man down in the Square who hid behind a tree, then a child, and finally a woman at East Broad and Bay. The cow was last seen by the police, who had orders to shoot to kill, "... moving with lowered head and straightened tail through the Red Light district."

These cows would sometimes get loose and run down Broughton clearing the street in minutes as shoppers would dash into stores and doorways. The cow would be chased by "policemen, boot blacks, idlers, and dogs." One such chase in 1896 ended with the cow leaving Broughton, taking a turn around the police barracks, then headed north on Abercorn and ended in Oglethorpe Square where he came to bay. Sergeant Linng then fired at him with his revolver, but finding that it only "maddened him further" obtained a Winchester from the barracks. He gave it to Mr. West, a member of the Georgia Hussars militia and a good shot, who ended the matter and then it was on to the butcher. It wasn't quite the O.K. Corral, but for a hot summer day in August it made for plenty of excitement.

Savannah suffered from the nation's alcoholic problem that swept through in the latter half of the 19th

Century leading to Ladies Temperance Societies and then Prohibition. It was common for the police to find both men and women passed out in the middle of the street late at night during their rounds. So one day in March 1872 the newspaper reported that before the Mayor's Court appeared:

> *"Martin Jury, a sorry looking specimen of human anatomy headed the column and was invited briefly to inform his Honor why he selected the sidewalk near Oglethorpe Square as a couch. Martin replied that his gastric organs are out of order and that he had been recommended to try "lager" for relief. Strange to say the beer, instead f settling in his gastronomic regions, mounted to his head, and wooed him to sweet repose. His Honor advised him to try other remedies not so potent and required ten dollars for the advice."*

As you follow Abercorn Street, near York Lane is the apartment where Shoeless Joe Jackson lived with his Savannah wife at 143 Abercorn. He was on a farm team here in 1909 which is no doubt how they met. He moved back to Savannah after he was banned from baseball in the Black Sox scandal. The scandal involved the 1919 World Series in which he led both teams in hits with 12. He could hardly be accused of throwing the Series when he led in many batting categories, yet he was. His career batting average of .355 is still third highest in all of Major Leagues. After being acquitted by a jury, yet still banned from playing, he moved to his wife's town of Savannah and met his Field of Dreams by opening a dry cleaning business.

Shoeless Joe Jackson

Continuing on you come upon Oglethorpe Avenue which represented the southern most line of Colonial Savannah's wooden palisade that encircled the town. The palisade touched the inside of the current Colonial Cemetery. The street was also called South Broad and sometimes "Under the Trees." The latter name was due to all the China Berry (Pride of India) trees planted in the middle with their interlocking limbs creating a shady bower over the street.

Across Abercorn from the D.A.R. entrance to Colonial Cemetery at the south west corner of Oglethorpe Avenue is the City Fire Headquarters at 121 Oglethorpe Avenue. Fireman's Hall containing a fire station was built there in 1854. After Lincoln was elected in November 1860, meetings were held around Savannah in support of South Carolina's secession including at Fireman's Hall.

Men gathered to hear patriotic secession speeches wearing secession cockades of palmetto leaves. The streets were filled with cheering thousands. Brass bands played, rockets soared and bonfires were ablaze. To many, like Colonel Charles Olmstead, the defender of Fort Pulaski, "the old town seemed to have gone crazy." The current building was constructed in 1937.

Colonial Park Cemetery

It started out as a cemetery for just Christ Church and was called the Christ Church Burying Ground. When the British retook Savannah in December 1778, General Elbert and his militia men sheltered in the cemetery as they were fired on by the British from the west. Elbert was fortunate to escape Howe's disastrous defense of the city as the British troops proceeded to bayonet then rob the fleeing civilians.

The cemetery was enlarged around 1795 and a high brick wall built around it. The wall stood for a hundred years before being mostly torn down in 1896 as the Cemetery was converted to a park.

Colonial Cemetery by Ebyabe

The last burial was in 1853, which was a good thing because by the end of November 1854 more than 650 Savannahians had died from the latest yellow fever epidemic and needed to be put somewhere. It was said that on the worst days the town's carpenters were unable to keep up with the demand for coffins. Fires of tar were lit throughout the city as the medical profession suggested it as a deterrent to the harmful *miasma*.

In an 1854 letter to the *Southern Christian Advocate* the pastor of the Methodist Church described the city:

How changed is our beautiful, growing, healthy city, lately full of enterprise, noise and business. Now it is nearly depopulated. The long streets are empty, save a few sad processions which are seen silently hastening on – there a long train of mourners – here a lone hearse bearing the dead to the city of silence. And at eventide in the public squares, the pride and beauty of the city, in place of the gay groups that promenaded the snow white walks, and the merry children that romped upon the green grass, there is a tar-fire flaming in the centre, throwing a lurid glare on the surrounding trees, and spreading abroad a long train of pitchy smoke that covers the city like a mourning veil.[1]

Northern cities had suffered terribly such as in the great Philadelphia yellow fever plague of 1793. Yet by the 1800s these epidemics seem to be mostly in Southern coastal towns with their nearby marshes and swamps and occasional excessive rainfall. Each of Savannah's epidemics was preceded by extraordinary heat and rains.

The current size of the cemetery is 6 acres and contains about 9000 graves. The Moravians, just as in Oglethorpe Square, have a small memorial here. Despite doing little, they left their mark.

The Jewish members of the city were not buried here as they had their own cemetery first at Oglethorpe and Bull and then Sheftall built one located off MLK Blvd. The Sheftall cemetery served as the fall back position when the French and Revolutionaries failed to take the British Spring Hill Redoubt. Most of the Sephardic members soon moved on to Charleston after arriving in 1735, but the Ashkenazi members stayed and were fervent patriots.

At some point the Cemetery allowed Catholics in and they were buried in the southwest portion. Later they were dug up and moved to the Catholic Cemetery on Wheaton Street (old Thunderbolt Road). Like the slave and Potter's Field graves, just because you've been buried once, doesn't mean you won't be again. It's a Savannah tradition!

In 1902 they discovered that the "saviour of the South from British tyranny" and that most famous son of Rhode Island, Major General Nathanael Greene's bones were located in the old Graham vault in Colonial Cemetery. They soon moved him and his son to the monument in Johnson Square. It's never over until we say it's over.

During the Union Occupation soldiers were tented in the Squares and in this cemetery. Some of the dates on the headstones were changed by bored Union soldiers so not all of the dates make sense. Some of these head stones are hung on the back wall near Perry Lane.

Funeral processions to the "Old Cemetery" were all on foot from the house. The only horse drawn carriage was the hearse, which was owned by the city. The Keeper of the Cemetery was called the Sexton and he was required to attend all funerals dressed in solid black clothes with black crepe over one arm. The order of the funeral procession had the Sexton walking in front holding his staff of office, then the horse drawn hearse pulling through the deep sand with three pall bearers on each side all in black dress, then members of the family, then relatives and friends and finally the servants. A New Orleans jazz band would have been nice, but jazz hadn't been invented yet.

Several famous Georgians are buried here including Button Gwinnett, signer of the Declaration of Independence, and General Lachlan McIntosh, who killed Gwinnett in a duel. The McIntosh Scottish Clan was brought over by Oglethorpe in 1735 to defend the Colony from the Spanish. Lachlan was a child at that time. My own McIntosh ancestor fought for the British during the Siege, but Lachlan fought for the Revolutionaries. In the south the Revolution was just as much a civil war among neighbors, as a fight against the British. As with any civil war, cruelty abounded and was personal.

Gwinnett was a failed businessman, but very popular with the people in Savannah. He and McIntosh quarreled over many things including who would lead a Continental brigade. Finally, the men's opposition came to a head. McIntosh's brother had been accused of trafficking with the British in Florida. This accusation was supported by the evidence. Lachlan didn't care and when Gwinnett repeatedly accused his brother McIntosh called him a scoundrel and Gwinnett challenged him to a duel.

They went down Thunderbolt Road, now called Wheaton Street, to a meadow owned by the temporarily ex-Royal Governor Reynolds. They separated by 12 feet, faced each and fired. Both were wounded. Gwinnett was shot above the knee which broke a bone and he crumpled to the ground. McIntosh was also shot in the leg, but only in the muscle. McIntosh asked Gwinnett if he wanted to have another go and Gwinnett brilliantly said he did, if someone would just lift him up! Then their seconds intervened and either said honor had been satisfied or maybe they said, "no this is dumb" and ended it. Then McIntosh walked over and he and Gwinnett shook hands. McIntosh's second was James "Pink House" Habersham.

Later Gwinnett died of gangrene due to poor treatment by his doctor. When McIntosh went to see Gwinnett's widow to explain, she told him she understood it was the doctor's fault! McIntosh had to flee Savannah after the duel and was transferred north to Washington's Continental Army. Lachlan's brother was not as fortunate and had his plantation house burned, crops destroyed and slaves confiscated and sold. He had to hide out in the swamps of coastal Georgia.

Throughout the 19th Century dueling was a common means of settling insults and disputes. During the Civil War Juliette "Daisy" Gordon Low's father fought a duel with his own sergeant who had insulted him. They used double barreled shotguns at thirty paces. Both survived.

Even the heroic Nathaneal Greene was challenged to a duel. A disreputable fellow named Gunn who Greene found to have wrongfully sold a Continental Army horse challenged him. To no surprise, Gunn the horse thief was later elected a U.S. Senator. Greene refused the challenge and so Gunn threatened a personal assault. Greene replied, "I always wear pistols and will defend myself."

The Habersham father and sons are all buried here as is William Scarborough, a major backer of the Steamship Savannah. His Scarborough House was made into a former slave children's school after the Civil War. It is on MLK, open to visitors and holds the *Ships of the Sea Museum*. When President Monroe visited Savannah in 1819 he was entertained at Scarborough's house.

Interestingly, Mr. George DeRenne of Wormsloe bought the Scarborough house after the Civil War in 1878 with the proviso that it be used as a school for African-American children. At the exact same time he paid for a bronze statue of a generic soldier to be placed above the monument to the Confederate dead in Forsyth Park. Mr. DeRenne was a strong believer in his community, black and white.

Habersham vault
Photo credit: The Historical Marker Database (HMdb.com)

The overlooked naval hero Captain Denis Cottineau (de Kerloguen) is also buried here. This fine Captain of the *Pallas* was part of John Paul Jones' small squadron operating off of France in 1779. Pallas was the Titan god of battle and war craft. As John Paul Jones famously engaged and defeated the frigate *Serapis*, while stating "I have not yet begun to fight," Cottineau's *Pallas* took on and defeated the sloop of war *Countess of Scarborough* and then tried to help Jones save his ship the *Bon Homme Richard*. He deserves our thanks. John Paul Jones went on to serve the Tsar of Russia while Cottineau briefly made his home here before dying of consumption in 1808.

One of Cottineau's sons grew up in Savannah, joined the priesthood and became a missionary in India. The other son, Achilles, tragically died, shot through the heart, in a duel with his good friend. The story is very odd in that the duel was fabricated to satisfy a problem his friend was having with another.

Also buried here is Father Jean (John) Le Moine, a refugee from the French Revolution and one of the first Catholic priests to minister in Savannah. In 1971 the French Ambassador to the United States laid a wreath at each of these Frenchmen's graves.

Some victims of the 1820 yellow fever, also referred to as "yellow jack," epidemic are buried in the cemetery. The epidemic took close to 800 lives, with approximately 600 being men. Dr. Warren gave several causes but the first was "[a] general epidemic condition of the atmosphere of extraordinary virulence, either proved to exist, or produced by an uncommon deficiency of the electric fluid." There you have it.

The population at the beginning of the plague was

close to 7,523, but at the end had dropped to only 1,494. The total population was equally divided between the races with over 500 being labeled "freed people of colour."

Savannah may not have known the precise vector of the disease, but it did know that having wet culture rice fields on both the east and west side was unhealthy. After this date Savannah took measures to change these areas to dry culture. When the next epidemic occurred in 1854 the blame was first ascribed to a ship from Havana then to dredged mud from the river. Just over a 1,000 died in that scourge immediately followed by a hurricane. Those that could afford it moved to their summer homes in the mountains or went up North until the first frost.

A few victims of the *Pulaski* are also here. The Pulaski was a steamship headed to New York with over a hundred Savannahians aboard. Off of Wilmington, N.C. one night in 1838 the boiler blew up and the ship broke in two. Some were saved and many were not. Hardly a Savannah household didn't have someone affected. The young Telfair sisters had tickets to go, but then discovered that a family they disliked was also going so they cancelled. That other family perished. Except for the fickle finger of fate, we might not have the Telfair Academy of the Arts, Hogdsen Hall or the Telfair Hospital.

Nathanael Green's granddaughter was also aboard and barely survived.

I could also relate some ghost stories if I dared. It is true that late at night, when the river fog rolls in "on little cat feet" and "sits looking over harbor and city on silent haunches then moves on" that things get spooky in the moonlight, both in the city and in this cemetery.

Walking beside Colonial Cemetery down Abercorn

toward Liberty Street, you cross Hull and Perry streets. These are named for two American naval heroes of the War of 1812.

Lafayette Square

Lafayette Square is located on Abercorn, between Harris and Charlton Streets. It was laid out in 1837 and is named for the Revolutionary War hero Marquis de Lafayette, who visited Savannah in 1825.

Harris Street was named for Charles Harris, Mayor from 1802-04 and who was a noted lawyer in the city. Charlton Street is named for Thomas Charlton, Mayor and Judge of the city who performed great services during the time of the 1820 yellow fever epidemic.

The Square contains a fountain commemorating the 250th anniversary of the founding of the Georgia colony. This fountain is dyed green for St. Patrick's Day, which is a big festival in Savannah and second largest in the country. The fountain is a beautiful piece of art. Look for the frogs!

Photo credit: SavannahGAVisitors.com

On this square are the **Andrew Low House**, **Hamilton Turner Mansion**, and the **Flannery O'Connor House**. Nearby is the Roman Catholic Cathedral of John the Baptist.

Photo credit: Savannah.com

The **Cathedral of St. John the Baptist** resides on the northeast corner of the square at East Harris and Abercorn streets. The Cathedral was in the opening scene of Disney's live film in 2019 of *Lady and the Tramp.* Its construction was completed in 1876. In 1898 a huge fire destroyed the entire Cathedral except the outside walls and spires. Originally the Georgia Colony's charter forbade Catholics from residing in the colony, but this prohibition was removed after the Revolution. The prohibition may have been because of the fear that Catholics would tend to sympathize with the Spanish enemy in Florida or because of the original antipathy toward Catholics by the Protestant American colonies.

The original congregation came from French planters fleeing the slave rebellion in Haiti. Ironically the Haitian slaves that led the rebellion served with the French in Savannah and fought for our independence against the British. A memorial to those Haitian soldiers is in Franklin Square. The Cathedral is in typical French Gothic style and is the oldest Catholic Church in Georgia. In 2003 a man waving a gun entered and set a damaging fire. He was confronted by Monsignor O'Neill, originally from County Tipperary, who yelled "Don't point that gun at me. I'll knock your head off."

Savannah has a large Irish population with many having ancestors arriving as immigrants building the Central Railroad from Savannah to Macon in the 1830's and 40's. This was the brainchild of Juliette Gordon's grandfather whose memorial is in Wright Square. The railroad had periodic financial difficulties and at one point during the national 1837 financial crisis could not pay the Irish. About 150 marched on the town demanding their pay. They were met at the Louisville road by some militia and two cannons. A Father O'Neill met the strikers and somehow resolved the situation. By 1860 out of 13,875 white inhabitants, 3,145 or 22.6% were Irish immigrants. Even my own family had an Irish servant girl named Lily who shows up in the 1860 Census.

At 321 Abercorn are the Lafayette condominiums. This building is on the site of the Octavus Cohen house. His daughter, Fanny, kept a two week diary beginning when Sherman came to town on December 21, 1864. Fanny was an ardent Confederate and railed against the Yankees. She complained as to how the Yankees stole their firewood during the cold days of December. Their house quartered General Hazen, whom they knew before the War and who had been in charge of capturing Fort McAllister. Her comment about him was "[h]e was very considerate of us during his stay and said nothing offensive."

The **Andrew Low House** at 329 Abercorn St. was built in 1848 by one of Savannah's wealthier merchants, Andrew Low II, on the site of the old jail. You can see the jail's location on the 1818 map below. It is the dot inside the top triangle of the fortifications under the word *City*. The fortifications shown here were from the War of 1812, which caused Savannah a great deal of anxiety.

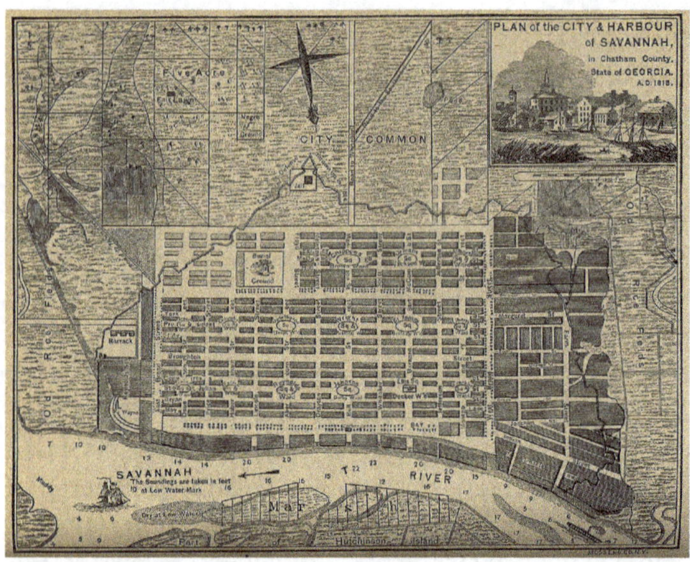

When the jail was closed in 1846, Andrew Low immediately bought the lot and built his fine house in Greek Revival style. Until the 1850's there was nothing beyond this house all the way to Gaston Street except a city common consisting of a broad grassy stretch of land. In the summer sportsmen would come out to the field in the evening and shoot night hawks.

The Low shipping firm had been in business for several decades and was very successful. Andrew Low II had taken over the business from his Uncle and expanded it. During the Civil War he engaged in some early blockade running and was arrested by the Union when he traveled back from England. He protested his innocence and was paroled which ended his active role in the War. While he lost a good deal of money locally, his English investments held up and he exited the War in better shape than most.

In 1855 the famed English writer William Makepeace

Thackeray stayed at the house. Low served as English Counsel so offered the famed author accommodations. He is the author of *Vanity Fair* and *The Luck of Barry Lyndon* which Stanley Kubrick (*2001*, *The Shining*) turned into a movie. The desk in the house where he wrote is still in one of the bedrooms. Thackeray complained about everything while he was in America. He was glad to take the money for his lectures, but a disagreeable person overall. He gave one lecture at the Savannah Theater calling it "a dirty little theater." Yet he always praised Low's hospitality and enjoyed the home's quiet nature allowing him to read and think.

Low House by Elisa Rolle

Robert E. Lee was a great friend of the family and godfather to one of the children. He had visited Andrew Low's wife's family, the Mackays, many times since his days supervising the construction of Fort Pulaski. Lee stayed at the Low house when he visited Savannah in 1870 at the age of 63. He had "snow-white hair and beard." He was not in good health as you can tell from this photograph that he made with General Johnston when he visited Savannah. Lee is on the right. He died a few months later. Sherman was right when he said, "War is hell," but it is also bad for your health.

Savannah actually made out pretty well from Union Occupation all things considered. The Occupation was led by the reasonable General Geary and Savannah was led by its Mayor, the reasonable and well educated Dr. Richard Arnold. The Mayor said in a letter

"Where resistance is hopeless it is criminal to make it." There were small incidences such as where ladies would refuse to walk under the United States flag hung outside the barracks (Desoto Hilton today), but also a lot of fraternization. By the time Sherman left to subjugate South Carolina in late January 1865, the City was well on its way to re-joining the Union.

Andrew Low's son William, known as "Willie," later owned the house. William doesn't seem to have done much of anything and was content simply to spend his inheritance. He married Juliette "Daisy" Gordon in 1886. Her family was worried about the marriage because Willie didn't seem all that stable, and as it turned out rightly so. William was not faithful to her and they were going through a long and convoluted divorce when he fortunately died in 1905. She founded the Girl Scouts here on March 12, 1912, and passed away in this same house in 1927 and was buried in her Girl Scout uniform. The Colonial Dames of Georgia owns the home and has lovingly restored it as a house museum.

Juliette "Daisy" Gordon

William Low's mother was Mary Stiles whom Andrew Low married in 1854. He was 22 years older than she. Mary's mother was from the prominent merchant family of Mackay. Donated to the house is the picture of the

Mackay ship, *The General Oglethorpe*, which was lost in a storm in 1802. An even more valuable donation was the Mackay breakfront, a Sheraton secretary made by the early cabinetmaker Joseph Barry of Philadelphia. Many letters by the Mackay family describing Savannah and events during the late 18th and early 19th centuries were written at this desk and can be read online.

During Andrew Low's time the house had a walled garden in back filled with camellias. The long windows had heavy dark green shutters, and in front, little iron balconies. If you made it up the stairs and past the red stone lions to see Mr. Low, old Tom, the butler would open the door for you. Mr. Low had a bit of a brogue and a red beard and visiting children would be scared witless by the old gentleman. In February 1904 the house was offered for rent and described as consisting "of 16 rooms, 3 bathrooms, and two dressing rooms...the drawing rooms have mahogany doors, French mirrors..."

Opposite the Low House and facing the Square is the **Hamilton-Turner Mansion**, now an Inn at 330 Abercorn. It is a Second Empire styled mansion built around 1873 by Samuel Hamilton. It was not originally stuccoed, but is now stucco over Savannah grey brick. After resigning his U.S. Navy Commission, Hamilton served under Colonel Lawton when Fort Pulaski was seized at the opening of the Civil War in January 1861.

The house may have been the first home to have electricity as Hamilton was the President of an early electric company and about 10 years after it was built he electrified the parlor. He was also President of a local bank. The house survived the fire of 1898 which destroyed the nearby Cathedral solely because it had a tin roof and not a wooden one. It played a small part in Berendt's book, *Midnight in the Garden of Good and Evil.*

Hamilton-Turner Mansion Photo credit: Savannah.com

Second Empire style is sometimes called French Second Empire and is noted for a Mansard roof which has two slopes on all four sides where the lower slope is steeper than the upper one. The style caught on with the robber baron wealthy in the north's gilded age, but it was expensive so the south did not have it very much. This may be the only full house of this style in Savannah. There are a few other mansard roof buildings around, but they are only bits and pieces of the style. The Rogers Mansion on Wentworth Street in Charleston is the only real example there as are the Saluda Cottages in Flat Rock, N.C. This style later became associated with spookiness so it was the house style on the old *Adams Family* and *Munster* television shows and Alfred Hitchcock's movie *Psycho*.

Hamilton had a stroke in 1898 and passed away. His widow turned the house into an apartment building renaming it the "Vendome." Vendome is a town in France where the river Loir turns into many arms. The apartments were only let to gentlemen and couples without children.

These houses on Abercorn were all part of what was called the "Elegant Eighties" of the 1880's. All the houses had a servant child whose purpose was to run notes all over town, as invitations and replies were thought too elegant for simple mail. The usual method was for several ladies to go in a carriage, with a boy on the box with the driver, and leave the invitations at the doors of those so honored. A story arose that one such lady remarked to the owner of a house she was currently visiting that her visiting list consisted of three parts, a first class visiting list, second class and third class, and that she was currently "out this morning visiting my second class list."

Young girls of a certain age could expect several callers on Sunday evenings. There was no such thing as dates. Sometimes if the maid or butler had their evening off, a gentleman would appear who was not favored. When the door opened he would ask, "Are the ladies at home?" and the young woman would reply *"No, the ladies are all out,"* and slam the door. To get to the beach at Tybee young couples would take the train. If a young couple missed the midnight returning train, the next day the whole town would rock with excitement.

As you leave Lafayette Square you cross Charlton Street. The **Battersby-Hartridge-Anderson** house at 119 E. Charlton was built in 1846 and is the only surviving Charleston designed house in Savannah. The main entrance was accessed through the yard and garden rather directly from the street. It is surprising that the two cities did not share more in architecture. William Battersby was a merchant and he lost his son at sea on a ship sailing from Liverpool to America during the Civil War.

At 207 E. Charlton Street is the birthplace and childhood home of one of America's greatest Southern writers, **Flannery O'Connor**. After Tennessee Williams, she is generally considered the South's finest writer. In contrast to William Faulkner, her writing is clean, crisp and concise. It is also Southern Gothic, which is a unique style all its own. Her home was built in 1855 and is open for visitors on some days. In her day the basement was used for storage, the parlor floor was the living area and the top two floors were bedrooms and baths.

O'Connor home by JRempel

When she was young she taught her chicken to walk backwards. There is an annual celebration of her life on the Square in March where this event is demonstrated. Her comment was, "[w]hen I was six I had a chicken that walked backward and was in the Pathé News. I was in it too with the chicken. I was just there to assist the chicken but it was the high point in my life. Everything since has been an anticlimax." Her best novels were *Wise Blood* and *The Violent Bear It Away*. Yet she is best known for her collection of Southern Gothic short stories in *A Good Man Is Hard to Find*. This collection is my personal favorite and should have won the National Book Award in 1956, but was a finalist. No one remembers any of the other books.

As you walk down Abercorn from Lafayette Square you cross the prettiest street in all of Savannah which is Jones Street. It is named for Major John Jones who died at the Siege of Savannah in October 1779. In the 1839 dedication the city said Jones "...fell within one hundred yards of the spot patriotically dedicated to his name, while fighting for the liberties of his country" and the city was "...grateful to one of its deliverers of this hemisphere from foreign thralldom." Savannah has never been short on hyperbole.

Bricks were a common paving method at this time to control the deep sand that made up most of the streets. Sidewalks were uncommon well into the 19th century. It was common at that time to see a tired horse pulling a carriage through these deep sandy streets as cascades of sand poured off the wheel rims. Under the asphalt paving in the historic district you will find the remnants of these bricks and cobblestones. Jones Street was never subject to such asphalt ignominy. At the south east corner of

Jones and Abercorn is the wonderful old breakfast eatery of **Clary's**, a favorite of locals.

There is a house on Jones that sometimes has a mysterious visitor. The television and water turn on in the middle of the night. The owners put in security cameras and hired a service. They get calls from the service when they are away saying there is movement in the house, but the cameras never show a human. The owners and ghost are both possessive of each other, so no names.

Some of these houses have side galleries to catch the breeze as they do in Charleston. One such house is on the corner of Abercorn and Taylor at 10 East Taylor. Built around 1880 its twin is across the street on the western side. The western house is called the Comer house as it was owned by Hugh Comer, President of the Central of Georgia Railroad. Jefferson Davis visited Comer here in 1886. Jefferson Davis was well acquainted with Savannah as his two daughters were educated at the Catholic girls' school here, St. Vincent's, while Davis was imprisoned after the Civil War. St. Vincent's Academy is still going strong.

Calhoun Square

This Square is located on Abercorn, between Taylor and Gordon Streets. The Square may have been built on top of an old slave cemetery and evidence suggests Charlton Street as being that cemetery's northern boundary. In 1855 all bodies were exhumed and placed in the new Laurel Grove Cemetery. Let's hope they didn't miss any.

The Square was laid out in 1851 and named for the South Carolina state rights advocate John C. Calhoun. Calhoun served as a Secretary of War, Secretary of State and was Vice President under Andrew Jackson. Taylor Street was named for General Zachary Taylor who was a hero of the 1846 Mexican-American War and later became President. Gordon Street is named for William Gordon, Mayor of the city and founder and chief promoter of the Central of Georgia Railroad that connected the port of Savannah to the cotton growing region of the middle of the state. He died young from over work and was Juliette Gordon Low's grandfather. His monument is in Wright Square.

Calhoun visited Savannah in 1819 as part of President Monroe's entourage when he was Secretary of War. He later fought with President Andrew Jackson in 1832 and threatened Jackson with the Nullification Ordinance whereby South Carolina could "nullify" any federal law it did not like. Foreshadowing the Civil War, Jackson's response was to pass the Force Act giving Jackson authorization to lead an army to South Carolina in order to compel compliance with federal law. Calhoun's divisive rhetoric and actions laid the groundwork for the secessionist position and the disastrous Civil War. His stance was very popular in both Georgia and South Carolina so he was honored with statues and parks both before and after the Civil War. He is not so honored now.

Almost all of the Square's original buildings are still extant. The old **Massie School** allows for visitors and illustrates how children were taught in olden days and has many exhibits. It was established by Peter Massie's 1841 bequest in his Will for a school for the poor white children of Savannah. It opened in 1856. Sherman turned it into a Union hospital during his occupation.

Massie by Elisa Rolle

In 1857 soon after Massie School opened, its classes were described as follows:

> *"The pupils are composed of boys and girls in nearly equal numbers. [T]here is at no time any communication between the sexes. They make their entrances and exits by different doors, have separate play-grounds..."*

Instruction was given in Natural Philosophy, Mathematics, Drawing, Latin, French (at extra cost) and vocal music. Natural Philosophy was a sort of Romanticism survey of the physical world before the study was later called science and divided into its many parts. Savannah was the first city south of Virginia to offer free education.

In the autumn of 1863, the 1st Georgia Volunteer Regiment consisting of several different militia groups including my great grandfather's 18th Battalion, Savannah Volunteer Guards, were brought back from their defense of Battery Wagner at Charleston. They encamped on the open ground behind Massie along what is now East Gordon Lane.

The house at 432 Abercorn was built by Benjamin Wilson in 1869. You may hear many odd stories about Wilson and this house. The truth though is much harder to find.

Wesley Monumental Church opened on the Square in 1878 and was built in the usual Romanesque-Gothic style. The builder that worked on the Hamilton-Turner house also worked on this church.

The cornerstone was laid in August 1875 with much ceremony. In it were placed a number of newspapers,

Confederate money, a 1779 Continental Bill, an ancient coin from the Macedonian Empire under Philip II (Alexander's father), a coin under Claudius Caesar A.D. 41, an 1871 California gold quarter dollar, and lots of other coins from around the world.

By the end of the 19th Century, each Square had acquired a distinct personality. They even had their own sport squads of young boys. In June 1888 the Calhoun Square "baseball club" defeated the Gwinnett Street "nine" by a score of 13 to 12. In January 1903 the Calhoun Square football team defeated Franklin Square 30-0. At Christmas time, such as on December 25, 1889, wooden barrels would be piled in the middle of each Square and lit in huge bonfires in an attempt to outdo each other. There would occur an occasional "barrel raid" on another Square's fire ending in "bruised noses and black eyes."

Each Square also had its own water pump and by 1887 complaints were constant. The paper said the water was a "fruitful source of income for doctors, druggists, and undertakers." It was acknowledged that the one in Calhoun Square "gives the best water."

At Abercorn and Gaston on the south west corner was built the *Marine Hospital* later called the *Savannah Hospital*. It was called the *Marine Hospital* because it originally dealt with sick seamen. Because these were thought to have contagious diseases the hospital was built far away from the city. Indeed, from this location to the Andrew Low House was simply an open common with few buildings.

Across Abercorn from this Hospital was a God's Acre or Potter's Field where the unknown dead seamen were buried. When Laurel Grove Cemetery opened in 1853 these bodies were exhumed and moved. Hopefully they found them all. The term "Potter's Field" is based on Mathew's Gospel that Judas returned the pieces of silver to the priests who then used the money to buy a piece of land in which to bury poor people. That land had previously been used to excavate pottery clay.

If you go west down Gaston Street, you will be headed toward Forsyth Park and the end of our Abercorn Street random walk. Of course, if you go east then you can begin your walk back up Habersham Street toward Whitfield Square.

At 126 East Gaston on the corner is a beautiful 1881 Italianate house. It has two large marble fireplaces and 14 foot ceilings. Jim Williams began to restore the house but then died, his death perhaps caused by the stress of his four trials for murder. The house is now owned by Savannah College of Art and Design.

If you walk around the hospital down Gaston toward Forsyth Park, you will see the grand old Candler Oak next to Drayton Street. It is over 300 years old and is protected by a fence. It is magnificent and bears witness to the birth and history of Savannah.

A Random Walk Down Habersham Street

Habersham Street was considered the last street of respectability in the city. The area beyond the street to the east toward the Old Fort area was reported by the police chief in 1855 to contain "one hundred liquor vending shops, twenty-six sailor boarding houses, and five large house of ill fame, besides numerous small ones..."

As you begin your walk down Habersham from Bay Street, take a peek down Bay Lane on your left toward Price Street. In this lane was a small house where Mary Woodhouse, a free woman and widow, secretly taught slave and free children how to read and write prior to the Civil War. She taught 25 to 30 pupils at a time, while always under threat of discovery. The remarkable Susie King Taylor was taught to read and write in this secret school for two years. She would arrive around 9 a.m. with her books wrapped in paper so a policeman or other white person could not see them. The students would go in the back gate, one at a time, into the kitchen which was the schoolroom.

Susie King Taylor in 1902 living in Boston

Interestingly, during the war Susie King Taylor joined Union troops on Hilton Head Island where she learned to fire and clean muskets. In 1864 she moved with this troop to the beach near Battery Wagner on Morris Island outside Charleston. Battery Wagner was where the famous 54th Massachusetts made a frontal assault in July 1863.

Their brave assault was the subject of the movie *Glory*. My great grandfather defended Battery Wagner with the Savannah Volunteer Guards until it was abandoned in September 1863. It currently lies under water as the sea proved to be the final victor.

According to her memoir, the Union would send shells into Charleston from Battery Wagner several times an hour. Outside the Battery "were many skulls lying about." "I have often moved them one side out of the path." "[B]y this time I had become accustomed to worse things and did not feel as I might have earlier in my camp life."

The likelihood that these bones were from the 54th Massachusetts is fairly high.

1890 Currier & Ives Illustration of 54th Massachusetts'assault on Battery Wagner

Warren Square

This first Square on Habersham was laid out in 1791 and is outside the hustle and bustle of Bull and Abercorn Streets. It is a more quiet, residential area and lies at the intersection of Habersham and East Bryan Streets. It was named for doctor and General Joseph Warren who was killed in the 1775 battle of Bunker Hill (Breed's Hill). Warren led his militia in the heaviest fighting and stayed even when out of ammunition. In the third and final assault by the British he was killed. The British dishonored themselves by desecrating his body.

Trumbull's famous 1786 painting of General Warren's death.

At 324-326 E. Bryan Street is the **Wylly House** built around 1800 by Colonel Richard Wylly. The Colonel was the Quarter-Master General for the Continental Line of South Carolina. His sister married James (Pink House) Habersham, Jr.

The related Stiles family moved into it after the Civil War from their house in old Yamacraw. Their coachman was Frank Stiles. He was George Stiles' body servant, born on the same day. Frank went off to war with George who was a member of the Savannah Volunteer Guards as was my great grandfather. Frank played the fife and drums for the unit. They were both at the terrible battle of Sailor's Creek, the last great battle of the Civil War. When they came home to the Yamacraw house the servants shut the door in their face thinking they were tramps as they were in bad shape and their clothes tattered to shreds. George's grandmother recognized him and let them in. Frank carried his former master up the stairs to his room saying simply, "we fought hard but we got beat."

Several houses have been moved here from other locations such as the **Epppinger House**. This house is located at the northeast corner and was built in 1820.

At 22 Habersham Street is the **Spencer Woodbridge House**, which was built for George Spencer in the 1790s. It is frame, not brick, as its location caused it to avoid Savannah's disastrous fires. At 24 Habersham Street is the **Mongin-Carswell House**, built for John Mongin in 1797. The house was originally located on another lot on the Square. During Savannah's 1876 yellow fever epidemic, it was used as a hospital.

Union troops quartered in this Square when Sherman visited in December 1864. In September 1887 many complaints were heard about the daily passage of a small group of seven cows and a sheep dog through the Square. They were let out in the morning to go to pasture then returned by the same path at night. The children have to "scamper away to get out of the path of the cows." A father loaded a shotgun with buckshot and vowed to shoot one of them if they continued to scare the children. By 1901 a trolley car would go through the Square and boys would use the area for baseball.

As you near Habersham and Broughton on the northwest corner is the **Major John Berrien House**. It has recently been wonderfully renovated by a descendant. It was the last important unrestored house in Savannah. Berrien was from New Jersey, but moved to Savannah shortly before the start of the Revolution and at the age of 16 served as aide-de-camp to General Lachlan McIntosh. He was at famous Valley Forge in the winter of 1777 and was severely wounded at the Battle of Monmouth the following year. He built this house in 1791.

Berrien House in the 1920s

The newly restored Berrien House

John Berrien was appointed Collector of Customs in Savannah as his reward for being on the winning side. He is buried in Colonial Cemetery, just a few blocks from his home.

Berrien's son, also named John, became a lawyer. He was elected to the U.S. Senate and was later appointed Attorney General by President Andrew Jackson. He was hired by Spain in the famous 1824 *Antelope* slave smuggling case. The *Antelope* had been caught off Georgia violating the 1808 prohibition against slave importation. The son argued against freeing the slaves telling the United States Supreme Court they belonged to Spain. Berrien's opponent was the famous Francis Scott Key who argued on behalf of the United States that all were free. In its Solomon-like Decision the Court ruled that some belonged to Spain and some were free. Those freed were later conveyed to Liberia.

During his failed presidential campaign in 1844 Senator Henry Clay was a guest at this house and gave a speech from the portico. Later Clay would author the great Compromise of 1850 that delayed the Civil War by a decade. John Berrien's son would live in this house from 1824 until his death in 1856.

Fanny Fall ran an upscale brothel directly across the street from this house. As was sometimes said, "one night with Venus, and a lifetime with mercury."

Columbia Square

Crossing Broughton and walking a block down Habersham is Columbia Square. This Square is a lot smaller than the original Squares down Bull and Abercorn. It represents an expansion of the original Oglethorpe plan. This Square was established in 1799 and contains a fountain from Wormsloe Plantation at Isle of Hope. There are massive oak trees at each corner. It is bracketed by State and York Streets. The Square contains the beautiful **Davenport house**, **Kehoe house**, **Francis Stone house**, and **Abraham Sheftall house.**

The **Davenport House** was built in 1820 in a mix of late Georgian and transitional Federal style and is on the northwest corner at 324 E. State Street. Its rescue from the wrecking ball by Savannah's "seven grandes dames" in the 1950's was the catalyst for the movement to preserve old Savannah. The house is owned by the Historic Savannah Foundation and is a house museum. It contains a nice collection of Chippendale and Hepplewhite furniture.

Davenport House
Photo by Jud McCranie

Isaiah Davenport built the home for his large family of ten children. He also owned 9 slaves. Davenport was a highly respected architect and builder. Some of the male slaves likely worked in his business and not in the house. He moved here from Rhode Island around 1800 and the house has Rhode Island elements. After his death in 1827 his wife Sarah decided not to rent the house out, but converted the home into a boarding house. It was sold to the Baynards of Hilton Head in 1840 who kept it until the family sold it to the Savannah Historic Foundation in 1955.

Davenport used elliptical arch motifs in several places including over the front door, gable and cellar. The house is two stories over a high basement with an attic. The entrance is reached by horseshoe stairs with an exquisite wrought iron rail. The interior hallway is bracketed by elliptical arches.

Isaiah's son Hugh was an officer in the Confederate Army. In March 1865 General Grover, who had taken over from General Geary and was a vindictive man, ordered all families of Confederate officers to leave Savannah during those very cold days. So Hugh's wife and children became refugees. Hugh's daughter, Anna, later became one of the founders of the United Daughters of the Confederacy.

Sherman was good friends with the Gordon family because Nellie's father and brothers were Union officers and her Uncle was General Hunter who commanded Union forces at Hilton Head. One of her brothers was killed in 1862. To confuse matters even more, she was personal friends with General Robert E. Lee as she attended balls at West Point when he was the Superintendent. But her husband rode with Confederate General Jeb Stuart and later Joe Wheeler and because of Grover's orders they had to leave Savannah.

Sherman actually made the arrangements himself to place the Gordons, including Daisy Gordon, age 4, the future founder of the Girl Scouts on a steamer to New York. From there Nellie Gordon took her family by train to her home in Chicago. Nellie, was a Kinzie whose grandfather built the first house on the site of what later became Chicago.

On the train the passengers began to sing the popular song "We'll Hang Jeff Davis to a Sour Apple Tree." The Gordon children then replied:

Jeff Davis rides a milk white horse
And Lincoln rides a mule
Jeff Davis is a gentleman
And Lincoln is a fool

Daisy then turned to her mother and said "they shouldn't hang Jeff Davis on a *sour* apple tree cause he's my Papa's friend. I wouldn't care if they hung him from a *sweet* apple tree, but they shouldn't hang him from a *sour* one."

Across from the Davenport house at 402 State Street is the **Francis Stone House** on the northeast corner of State and Habersham. This federal style home was built in 1823. Stone was born in 1789 and was an arms dealer specializing in muskets. He was also a city alderman and was praised for his service during the 1854 Yellow Fever Epidemic.

Also on the Square is the **Abraham Sheftall House** at 321 E. York Street on the southwest corner built in 1818. It was moved here from Elbert Square when that Square was being destroyed to make way for a road. It is a three-bay frame house with a central chimney. The Sheftall family arrived in Savannah on the second ship in 1735. They were strong supporters of the Revolution and were imprisoned by the British under horrific conditions.

Unique in old Savannah at 123 Habersham Street is an interesting home called the **Kehoe House** built in 1892. It is a mix of styles some might call Revival, but contains some Italianate features as well. The cast iron Corinthian columns were made at Kehoe's foundry. The house is made of red brick with terra cotta moldings.

Kehoe House by Ebyabe

William Kehoe was an Irish immigrant who came to Savannah in 1851 with nothing and made good in the iron trade and had a very successful foundry called Kehoe's Iron Works. He was in the Confederate Army and fought at Gettysburg. He passed away in 1929. He was one of the main promoters of the railroad to Tybee. Kehoe lived here with his wife and ten children. At one time Jets quarterback Joe Namath bought the house for investment purposes.

There was a dispute about some of the home's construction bills and it went to a jury in 1893. The attorney opposing Mr. Kehoe made some reference to Shylock and Mr. Kehoe in his closing argument. Kehoe took offense at this and interrupted him. The attorney took a swing at him so Kehoe took a swing back. The court was not amused and fined them both.

Occasionally Kehoe had union troubles at his foundry. Once a group of men marched to his house and burned him in effigy. He then walked out of his house and stood in the middle of them and said "Go home lads, you've had your fun. Have a good supper, say a prayer for me, and be at work on time in the morning."

On the southeast Trust Lot is a yellow house in federal style and next to it a gray Italianate one with lovely iron work and bracketed cornices. Savannah's historic nature was under direct attack in the 1950's and 60's. The result of that attack is illustrated by the pitiful ugly one story cement building on the northeast Trust Lot. Not only is it of suburban utilitarian design, but it also does not face the Square.

As you walk south down Habersham you will cross Oglethorpe Avenue, formerly South Broad and the edge of town. You can spy Colonial Cemetery from the corner. Across Oglethorpe is the old police headquarters, which is also still the current one, but it's old and it leaks. The building was constructed in 1887. In front are some old police cars. They always remind me of the television show *Car 54, Where Are You?* Behind the headquarters is the old city jail.

In June 1923 they had a riot in front of the jail. The police had picked up a fellow and a mob was after him. The Governor declared martial law stating that Savannah "was in a state of insurrection." So a mob appeared in front of this jail. At 1 pm Major Moore declared that he was going to clear the streets. "They paid no attention to him." He opened fire with his men, shooting high. "To his surprise the mob responded shot for shot..." Firemen played a stream of water on the mob and they finally dispersed. The mob tried again that night and so the next day the militia unit, the Georgia Hussars, began patrolling the area. The militia was stationed behind machine guns and breastworks. They walked the perimeter with bayonets and wore trench helmets. All was quiet on the Habersham front.

Troup Square

Continuing our walk we cross over Liberty Street. This part of Habersham street gets very little traffic, whether tourist or local. It's just sort of out of the way. Ahead of us lies Troup Square, a rather smaller Square named after a Georgia Governor and Senator with Creek Indian family ties. He was also descended from the McIntosh clan that Oglethorpe recruited in 1735 to fight the Spanish.

Troup Square was established in 1851 and lies between Charlton and Harris Streets and is bisected by Macon. In the middle is the odd Armillary Sphere based on an old Greek celestial calendar. It serves as a sundial and was built in 1968. Portugal's flag has one too. The reason it is here is because the benefactor who funded the restoration of the Troup area wanted it here.

The Square also has a reproduction of the Myers dog water fountain. Mayor Herman Meyers was one of Savannah's better Mayors and served several terms around the turn of the 20th Century. Mayor Meyers gave the dog fountain to the City in 1896 and it was originally placed in Forsyth Park. Also facing the Square are homes on Kennedy Row built in 1872 and McDonough Row built in 1882.

Savannah held the Olympic Yachting competition in

1996. The Olympic Torch passed through Troup Square as it made its way through Savannah.

The boys of Troup Square had a rivalry with those in Madison Square. At Christmas 1892, a huge bonfire was lit in the middle of Troup and fireworks were given to the boys by the Mayor who lived nearby. As soon as the Mayor left, the boys went over to Madison and several fights broke out. It was claimed that the police didn't see a thing. Because baseball had become all the rage, Troup Square had its own team of boys and on July 5, 1888, they defeated the Georgias at Tybee in front of the Ocean house with a large crowd in attendance. They must have had a pretty good team because in April of that year they beat the Greene Square boys.

Whitfield Square

The last Square on Habersham is Whitfield. It was also established in 1851 and is between Taylor and Gordon Streets. It is named for the Reverend George Whitefield who founded Bethesda Orphanage in 1740.

This was the last of the City's Squares. To the city's shame, Oglethorpe's Plan was not continued beyond this Square. Surprisingly his Plan did appear once more in the early 20th Century in a suburban development called Ardsley Park where the parks are like diamonds on a street necklace enhancing the lives of the residents and their children.

Whitfield Square has a beautiful gazebo in the middle and many weddings are performed in the Square under its towering oaks with their swaying gray beards.

Whitfield Square Gazebo
Photo credit: Savannah.com

The area around Whitfield is noted for its Victorian and Queen Anne architecture. The Square also has two historic African-American Churches and may be the location of an old slave and freed people's cemetery.

Savannah prior to the Civil War

I thought I would give you some glimpse of Savannah prior to the Civil War from 1835 onward. The only American coinage in Savannah at the time was a large copper penny. All silver coins were British and prices of goods were quoted in that coinage. Firemen did not have horses for their wagons so would pull the wagons through the deep sand streets by hand using a rope. Every house was required to have a fire bucket for each fireplace.

The city was protected by a night guard with the Guard House at President and Whitaker streets. They were not in any uniform, but wore their everyday clothes. They carried a musket, blank cartridges, a rattle and a short club. The Guard House had a belfry with a bell that rang out at night announcing curfew. The night watchmen were required to call out the hours of the night such as "past ten o'clock and all is well." If a fire was sighted, the bell would ring, watchmen would run through the streets yelling "Fire! Fire!" and shoot their muskets and spring their rattles. Later the fire bell would ring in the Custom House belfry and could be heard across town with a "dismal boom" frightening all the little children asleep in their beds.

The young children were cared for by their nurses or maumas. The nurses would wear gingham frocks, white aprons and bright bandanna handkerchiefs, wrapped turban-like about their heads, with the ends tied in a bow like rabbit ears. There was a complete absence of baby carriages. Children not old enough to walk would be carried on their heads in baskets. Those who could crawl had higher baskets so they couldn't get out, but instead would peer over the top, squeal and pound their rattles. The nurses would just toss the basket on their head, balancing it as if it were laundry as they walked along.

In the late 1830's young men would join together to drink and sing songs. Some favorites were "Vive L'Amour," which is still sung occasionally, and "Landlord Fill the Flowering Bowl." Both of these originated as British drinking songs.

In the 1850's Savannah's young people danced to their favorite reels played on fiddles. "Billy in the Lowground" and "Camptown Races" were both favorites and you can still hear them played today. The young proclaimed their independence by following the lyrics of the "The Boatmen's Dance" and sang:

"Dance all night til broad daylight
And go home with the girls in the morning"
Like the last few years before Peal Harbor, they frolicked before the unforeseen dark and bloody future that would take these boys lives before their time.

A New Years custom of visiting was also observed. Carriages of young men would start at either the northern or southern part of town then go street by street calling upon every lady of their acquaintance. The parlors would be darkened, the lady in her best frock, gas light lit and refreshments laid out on a table awaiting the crowd. If it was not convenient for the lady to receive, then a basket for cards would be hung on the front door.

Young ladies would stroll along the *west* side of Bull Street toward Forsyth Park. The *east* side was where the Barracks (now Desoto Hilton) was located so was to be avoided.

Disease and death were constant companions in 19th century Savannah. Women faced childbirth with both joy and trepidation. Colonel Olmstead of the later Fort Pulaski command lost both his sister of 18 and his father to the Yellow Fever Epidemic of 1854. He was in military school outside Atlanta and was told not to come home "… as everyone was flying from the city who could."

Savannah after the Civil War

In the immediate Occupation years of 1865 and 1866 Savannah women became creative in acquiring what "greenback" money was available from the Occupiers. Several became pastry cooks and profitably sold their concoctions to the soldiers. One Irish woman reportedly sold some home-made hooch that could "kill in forty minutes at fifty yards."

After the War came the "Striving Seventies." The decade opened with one of the last duels in Savannah and this time it was over a sailing race. The contestants disliked each other so much that they fired four shots at each other although the Code Duello only allowed for two. They then tried a fifth shot which was fatally successful. While the winner was arrested, there was no indictment. I remember as a young boy my father inherited a set of dueling pistols from this era. Fortunately, he never had to use them and I never found them.

In April of 1870 General Lee and his daughter Agnes came to town and the City's joy overflowed. When he died in October the bells tolled the entire day, businesses were ordered closed and the city council draped in black.

The Seventies was a decade of rebuilding and improving. Complaints were made about it no longer being proper for housewives to beat their carpets in the Squares. Orchids were out of style as circumstances had made everyone poorer, but violets freshly picked were often given to a lady friend. Promenades for women began on the right hand side of Bull Street near Christ Church and extended to Forsyth. The area above along Bay and Factor's Walk belonged to the use of men and their business.

Older women dressed in black mourning clothes every day. Some wore long crepe veils down to their heels. The very elderly would reminisce constantly about family members and life from the antebellum past. For them life had stopped. For the younger women with children to support they could not afford to retreat into the past. War widows took in boarders to support their families. Others constantly made and remade their clothes. Lost fortunes and lives caused the older generation to pass on at a high rate. One woman who came into adulthood in the 1880's would recount her grandmother as having a "lined face and hopeless eyes" recounting the losses. Yet the "Striving Seventies" moved Savannah forward as it tried to recover. It could do no less.

Savannah became a theatrical town with many more plays and operas showing up than before. Minstrels and circuses were unending and even Buffalo Bill made an appearance.

The streets were generally unpaved sand with a few planks and cobblestones on some.

In 1876 Savannah was again devastated by the last of its yellow fever epidemics. One branch of my own family lost a small child to it causing them to move away permanently. The disease came in the summer after torrential rains. The rains filled the graves so that coffins had to be held down with poles until enough dirt could be placed on top.

After the "Elegant Eighties," described previously, came the "Gay Nineties" and the bicycle, which led to the emancipation of women. A woman could not ride in skirts that swept the ground so they became indecently high, to the ankles no less! She could not ride in leg-of-mutton sleeves against the wind so shirt-waists became in vogue along with small hats. Savannah was styling! The favorite song of the young at this time was "Daisy Bell (Bicycle Built for Two)." In September 1894, 24-year-old Annie Londonderry set out from Chicago with a change of clothes and a pearl-handled revolver to become the first woman to cycle around the world.

In the post-War period of the 1870's Savannah developed street cars. These were first drawn by horses and then around the turn of the century were electrified.

A SAVANNAH SCENE IN THE PIONEER DAYS OF THE STREET CAR
From a photograph in the collection of Mrs. Craig Barrow.

In the history of the street car in Savannah one of the best known conductors was Alexander M. Barbee. This photograph, taken in the 1880's, shows him on the platform (central figure) of a horse car which he drove on its regular route from the City Exchange to Thunderbolt. Mr. Barbee moved to the Isle of Hope about 1890, and was a conductor on that line for twenty years, retiring in 1914 to give full time to his Terrapin Farm, a successful industry established by him in 1904.

The Conductor shown here standing center on the platform in this 1880's photograph is Alexander Barbee. He founded a diamond terrapin turtle farm at Isle of Hope that his family ran for almost 80 years. I remember as a child looking down into the large mud pit swarming with thousands of diamond terrapins and scared I might fall in and be eaten! His terrapins were shipped to New York's Fulton Market at the corner of Beekman and Front streets. From there they traveled to Manhattan's finest restaurants for soup, as it was considered the Viagra of its day. It worked better than monkey glands he said. Prohibition sent the terrapin market into decline because it prevented using the essential ingredient of Sherry for the soup.

Alexander Barbee loved music boxes and Williams Jennings Bryan, the Presidential candidate and later Scopes Trial prosecutor. In 1911 he went to Washington, D.C. and walked up to Mr. Bryan and just handed him a terrapin egg. Mr. Bryan was very confused. But in about a minute the egg hatched and out crawled a baby turtle. That turtle, named Toby, went everywhere Mr. Barbee went as he kept him in his pocket. He trained the turtle to wink every time he asked it if it was time for a drink!

During the boom years of the 1920's, Savannah was ranked by the federal government as one of the nation's 30 most immoral cities. And proud of it! The city allowed legalized vice as a revenue raising measure. Anyone could operate a brothel as long as they paid the license fee. To appease voters who were shocked at such behavior the city also passed an anti-jazz ordinance prohibiting "lascivious music." Savannah has never had a problem being all things to all people. The city even had a Jazz Inspector who proclaimed that any dancing "...that brought into play that part of the body from the waist up….[is] a violation of the anti-jazz ordinance." This ordinance did not last long.

Many Georgia counties were dry, but Savannah never succumbed to that fate until Prohibition. Even after Prohibition was passed, Savannah, like Charleston, was mostly "wet." Smugglers were heard on their boats at Tybee, Isle of Hope, Beaulieu and in dozens of other creeks bringing in their loads from waiting ships. This is why Savannah became a foreign Scotch whiskey town and never a Bourbon one.

I hope you have enjoyed these random walks down Abercorn and Habersham with their separate flavors of history. We don't ask if "these walls could talk," but rather if these gray beard oaks in the Squares could tell their story.

About the Author

John H. Maclean has been a lawyer, Judge and author, but always in love with history. His family has been in Savannah since 1735 and in South Carolina since 1685.

CPSIA information can be obtained
at www.ICGtesting.com
Printed in the USA
LVHW061305290321
682828LV00027B/414